# Walkways and Drives:

## Design Ideas for Grand Entrances

Tina Skinner

Schiffer Publishing Ltd

4880 Lower Valley Road, Atglen, PA 19310 USA

Courtesy of Vengeance Creek Stone

Library of Congress Cataloging-in-Publication Data

Skinner, Tina.
Walkways and drives : design ideas for grand entrances / by Tina Skinner.
p. cm.
ISBN 0-7643-1360-6 (pbk.)
1. Garden walks. 2. Driveays. I. Title.
TH4970 .S5524  2000
717--dc21
00-013142

*Title page:* Courtesy of Bomanite Corporation

Designed by Bonnie M. Hensley
Cover design by Bruce M. Waters
Type set in Exotc350 DmBd BT/Korinna BT

ISBN: 0-7643-1360-6
Printed in China

Published by Schiffer Publishing Ltd.
4880 Lower Valley Road
Atglen, PA 19310
Phone: (610) 593-1777; Fax: (610) 593-2002
E-mail: Schifferbk@aol.com
Please visit our web site catalog at **www.SCHIFFERBOOKS.COM**

In Europe, Schiffer books are distributed by Bushwood Books
6 Marksbury Avenue Kew Gardens
Surrey TW9 4JF England
Phone: 44 (0) 20-8392-8585; Fax: 44 (0) 20-8392-9876
E-mail: Bushwd@aol.com
Free postage in the UK. Europe: air mail at cost.

This book may be purchased from the publisher.
Include $3.95 for shipping. Please try your bookstore first.
We are always looking for people to write books on new and related subjects.
If you have an idea for a book please contact us at the above address.
You may write for a free catalog.

# Acknowledgments

One need only read the rich resource guide at the back of this book to see who contributed to this project. It's a wonderful mix of manufacturers, industry organizations, and talented contractors and landscape designers.

Courtesy of Portland Cement Association

# Contents

# Introduction

An expanse of concrete pavers set in a traditional herringbone pattern and pigmented brick red reflects the quality of the home beyond.

Fantastic things are happening in the decorative paving industry. Those old cracking cement slabs are a thing of the past. New technology has increased the durability of paving materials, and advances in coloring and imprinting techniques for concrete and asphalt make it possible to imitate virtually look– inexpensively. You might not be able to afford bluestone or slate, or maybe there are no bluestone or slate quarries within hundreds of miles – but you can have that look.

Hardscaping is a major part of your home's design. The most permanent impression you make when designing your front lawn is the driveway, entry walk, landing or front porch, and even the retaining walls used around flower beds and in containing steep hills. Few people consider these elements that are so crucial to curb appeal for a home.

The most important rule of thumb in designing your front yard is finding what you like. That's what this book is for. Here are dozens of photos to thumb through, hundreds of design ideas to help you "hardscape" your environment. You can choose colors, textures, and shapes that appeal to you, as well as study furnishings and features that you'd like to incorporate in your outdoor environment. You'll see a broad sampling of both new and old materials, from high-tech concrete hardening and coloring agents to classic, quarried stone, and learn the language you need to discuss these materials with designers and contractors.

If you want to initiate the neighborhood's most talked-about home improvement project, we've got lots of ideas for you. Here are design ideas that announce, upon arrival, that this house is a step above the rest.

However, if you're watching your wallet, don't be daunted by the showplaces featured here. There are also simple ideas.

These images will prove invaluable to people building their own home, who want to start off right. Even if you can't afford a driveway of pavers right away, you can lay the foundation for it with your architect and contractor by leaving an appropriate concrete base to be capped in the future. If you're building a $500,000 home, you don't want a simple, straight walkway in the front, laid a mere two feet from the home. You want to add elegance with a curve or two, leave space for beautiful landscaping. These photos will help you pick a look that's right for your home, right for your lifestyle.

There are "hardscape" ideas to help tame and negotiate uneven terrain, or to maximize one's view of it.

Use this book to help you visualize the entryway you want. Study colors and textures so you'll know what to look for when you go shopping; terminology so you'll know how to talk to your contractor. Use the resource guide to help you find the right manufacturer or installer to meet your needs. Properly installed, your new patio should serve you for many years.

Two sizes of pavers create a pleasing grid, while their color mirrors that of soft stucco in this tile-topped Southwestern home.

A darker grid pattern was laid out for this diagonal pattern of square pavers.

Pressed concrete was used to create parking and patio areas for this home. The concrete was colored to mimic roof tiles and fieldstone found in the chimneys.

Courtesy of IXL Industries, Ltd.

This curving wall provides many functions for the homeowner. For one, it offers a level of privacy for the front of their home, while still leaving them visual access to the street. Built-in planters allow for greenery within the parking area, and provide built-in seating and a comfortable working height for the gardener.

A close-up shot shows the rounding effect created by tumbling pavers, here in traditional brick tones for this handsome stucco home.

Three different areas of imprinted concrete were used to create this impressive drive-up.

A broad entry walk/patio was created with a stunning fan pattern stamped in concrete that was tinted to resemble stone.

Courtesy of Sterling Landscape

This walk links a multi-level deck with an inviting back garden.

Patterned concrete creates barefoot-friendly walkways, patio, and parking areas for this beach home.

Courtesy of Portland Cement Association

# In Imitation

The following pictures illustrate the possibilities available to the home-owner today. From artistry with the real article – quarried stone, to the imitations available in concrete and asphalt. The colors and textures are exciting, and best of all, affordable!

Stencils were used to create this amazing imitation of mortar set bricks. The barely visible horizontal joints are the only giveaway, placed in the concrete slabs to allow for expansion and contraction.

This looks like stone, but it's actually stenciled concrete sprinkled with several tones of color hardener to create what looks like natural variation. There's a beautiful contrast with the natural aggregate sidewalk it crosses.

Rich colors were used, applied over stencils on wet concrete, for this walkway.

Courtesy of Aartcrete, Inc.

**TOP LEFT:** The look and feel of natural stone was created for this driveway using stencils and color hardeners. Note how the pattern was continued over curved surfaces at the end of the drive.

**BOTTOM LEFT:** A courtyard effect is created in front of this unusual home, accented by a cutout flowerbed. The herringbone brick surface is actually stenciled concrete.

Here's the look so many people are after – real stone. A true craftsman created this sun symbol from a cut center stone and natural "rays."

Sometimes called "European Fan," this pattern was created not in stone but using stencils and color hardeners.

Courtesy of Artcrete, Inc.

This homeowner wanted the effect of stone on their driveway, without ripping out the old driveway to accomplish it. Instead, a cement overlay was applied using stencils to completely alter the appearance of this now-impressive entryway.

The tint in this concrete is its first call to compliment. The next thing you'll notice is the texture.

**LEFT:** Cast-in-place concrete with the look of slate flagstones creates a wide drive, with scattered yellow to key in with the home and garage.

**CENTER:** A basic driveway would have been an understatement to this home of fieldstone. So faux stone was created for both the driveway and the patio/back entrance area. The effect was achieved with tinted, stamped concrete. Borders and pattern changes were used to indicate different use areas.

**RIGHT:** This is concrete, colored and placed so cleverly it would fool all but the most careful observer. A stencil was laid on wet concrete to create the web of "mortar" while pigment was applied in a variety of complementary hues to the "flagstones" in between.

23

A golden drive and walkway create an enchanting entrance for this home. The effect of natural stone was creating using stamped, pigmented concrete.

Courtesy of Portland Cement Association

Stamped asphalt creates the effect of random stone for this pleasing approach to a Southwestern home.

An asphalt walk takes on the character of a stone lane, with stenciled stones and sealers that add color.

Courtesy of Streetprint™

These gray flagstones are actually asphalt, stamped while hot and sealed with an acrylic-polymer coating for color.

Courtesy of Streetprint™

Courtesy of Streetprint™

An elaborate entryway was installed for a restaurant entrance, punctuated in the center by a stylized rose. The triangle petals were hand cut. The dark brown Pices Paver™ are among several shapes patented by artist Giuseppe Abbrancati.

# The Details

Courtesy of Gappsi™, Inc.

So beautiful, it could even draw one's eye from the seaside view, a stylized rose was created using hand-cut pavers for this restaurant patio.

An asphalt driveway gets traffic-stopping detail, with a custom address imprint and the effect of terra-cotta tiles.

This driveway looks like it was created with two tones of pavers, but was in fact done with an imprinting technique on asphalt. Acrylic-polymer sealers were used for color.

A long asphalt driveway is broken up with the insertion of several "paver circles." These circles are, in fact, a stamped effect created when the asphalt was hot and finished with colored sealers.

# Circular Drives

Gray imprinted concrete gives a feeling of flagstones to create an awe-inspiring entrance to this home, with a circle drive in front, and wrap-around drive to a rear entrance.

When seen from a distance, the "European Fan" pattern of pavers creates a graceful, scale-like appearance for this circular drive.

Courtesy of Bomanite Corporation

Imprinted concrete in an ashlar slate pattern creates an additional wow factor on entry into this grand property.

Mixed colors in the pavers creates an impression that this circular drive has been in place for years.

A bold dark and light color scheme mirrors the
contrasting trim of the home.

Retaining walls define this inviting entrance walk of
imprinted concrete.

Rich, earthy rock in the home and retaining walls are enhanced by imprinted and colored concrete caste in stone color and texture for the driveway.

Tumbled pavers create the impression that this parking area came with the house a hundred years ago. Beyond, a two-tone brick entry patio invites guests to step up in style.

**OPPOSITE PAGE**
Duo-tone pavers add interest to a circular driveway.

A stone fountain sculpture dominates this circular drive/ parking area, creating a dramatic entrance for a fine home.

Concrete was pressed in two patterns and a slight variation in tone to create interest for this drive/entryway.

A wide swath of brick pavers (made more looming by a wide-angle lens) loops in front of this Colonial-style home.

Here's a classic circular entrance. Your friends and family will call it brick, but technically it's paving stones – stones created from concrete and specially formulated to withstand ground contact for many years to come.

A sumptuous effect was created here with rising layers of concrete leading to the door. Alluvial stone was pressed into the spoke-pattern drive.

A spacious driveway is enhanced with two contrasting tones of colored concrete stamped along the border to resemble fish-scale pavers.

Strips of grass set within an imprinted concrete driveway add class and character to this wonderful, sweeping entrance. Capped stone pillars and a magnificent arched doorway complete the neo-classical effect.

A slightly darker hue is used for a center line to help direct traffic around this home. Semi-circle extensions into the lawn add interest.

A perfectly round driveway made of cast-in-place concrete adds architectural juxtaposition to this rambling rancher, and helps to direct traffic.

A wide-angle camera lens enhances the drama of this circular drive, but it is equally impressive in real life.

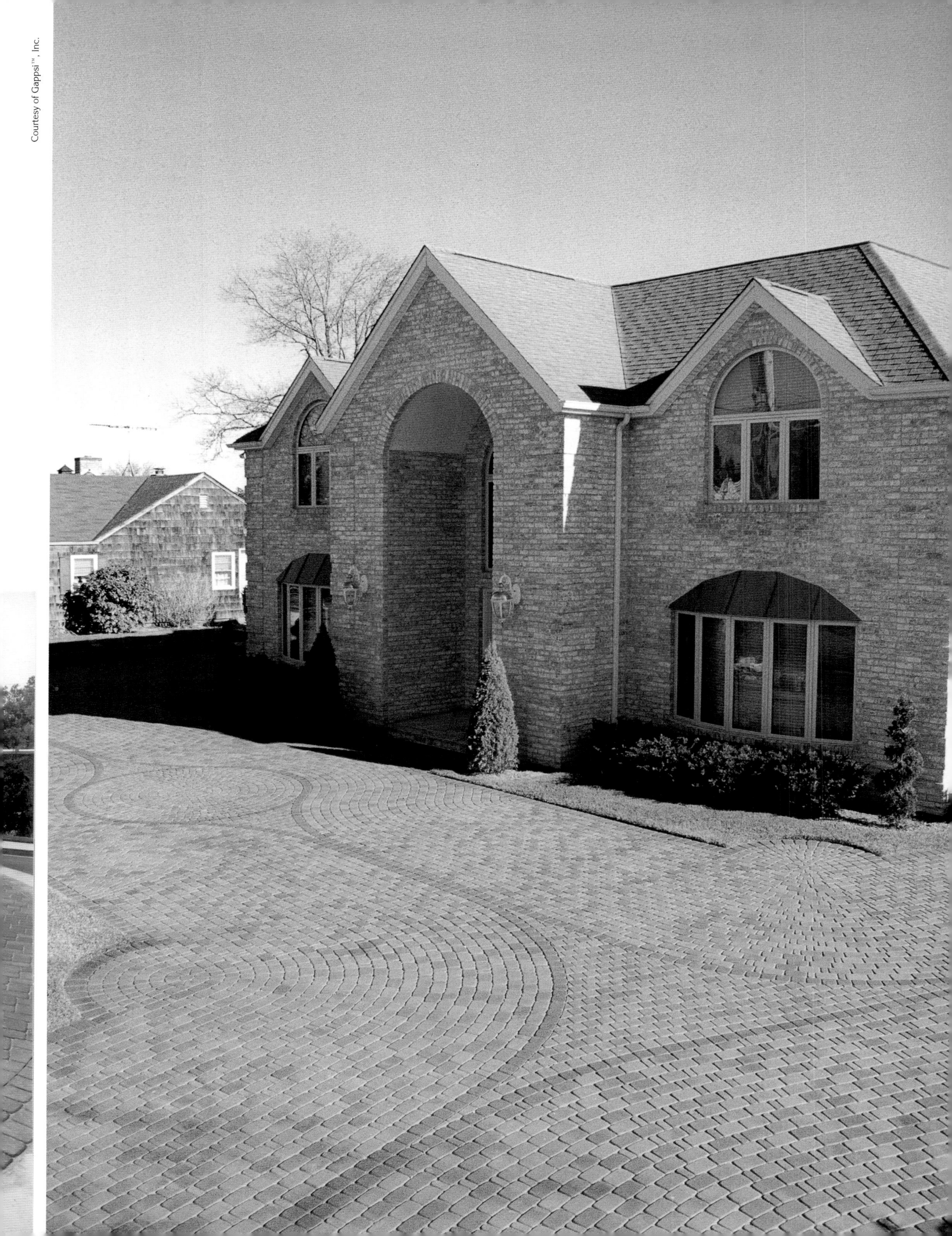

Courtesy of Gappsi™, Inc.

Deep-colored borders define the driving and parking areas in front of a home and garden that were designed to blend in with the surrounding countryside.

Two sizes of pavers break up the herringbone pattern in this expansive driveway.

Courtesy of Unilock

An asphalt entryway was dressed up using two sealer colors and an imprinting technique to replicate the look of hand-laid brick around the light post and at the entryway.

A classic cactus marks the center of a grand circular drive, created using Keyloc-shaped light gray pavers.

Courtesy of Superlight Block

Stencils were used to create the impression of inlaid brick pavers for this elegant circular driveway. Color hardeners are responsible for the two tones.

A flagstone effect was created for this expansive circular driveway and the road to the garage beyond using stenciled concrete.

# STRAIGHT SHOTS

Keylock-shaped pavers cut a swath through the rocky desert to this sprawling stucco home.

Simple in design, elegant in presentation – a herringbone driveway and walk create a conversation piece in the neighborhood.

Diamond insets and a dark border add interest to a heavy-duty herringbone pattern of pavers – proven to be the strongest brick formation for bearing weight.

A doublewide driveway gets added architectural interest, using pavers to create three alleyways.

Square pavers were mortared here for a beautiful grid-pattern drive and walkway.

Smooth and patterned concrete are juxtaposed for interest and texture in this three-car wide driveway.

Courtesy of Portland Cement Association

A big medallion in this drive adds interest and helps break up a big expanse of pavers.

Matching end slabs and an imprinted fish-scale pattern stamped in concrete form an impressive driveway.

Courtesy of Bomanite Corporation

64

# Adding Color

**LEFT:** An intricate pattern was created for this circular drive and walkway.

**BELOW:** Tri-colored pavers were lined up for a bright entrance to this home.

Rich charcoal gray-colored imprinted concrete mimics a custom garage door and light post.

An interlocking fan pattern was laid in pressed concrete, with two colors to add variety and interest.

Inset squares in complimentary colors break up this great expanse of driveway and walk, and add architectural interest. The project won a Unilock award for excellence.

This geometric sunburst pattern was put together using two shapes of pavers, with a huge payoff in design interest.

Hot asphalt was imprinted to create the look of hand-laid pavers, and two tones of sealers were used for decorative effect.

The look is like pavers, but this cost-saving driveway was crafted from asphalt using an imprinting technique and two tones of acrylic-polymer sealer.

This tri-colored cross pattern draws constant compliments for these homeowners.

Slate gray and brick red colors are used to break up and enhance an expansive driveway/parking area.

# Throw Them a Curve

Sunny terra-cotta colored pavers march in a straight line through an artfully curved drive and walkway.

Carefully inlaid nightlights add an element of safety, and highlight the golden glow of home and driveway.

These cement pavers were cast for their future role in creative, curving sidewalks and drives. Here a circle inset as well as a deep border create a path for the front door.

Courtesy of Portland Cement Association

Weathered paver "cobblestones" are the perfect choice for this entrance to a rambling spread of home, garage, and barn.

Keystones are contained by like-colored brick pavers set in two perpendicular rows for decorative flair.

Earth-toned pavers tie in with a brick facade on the home.

A small circle adds variation and color keys to a like-colored "brick" border. In fact, though, this entryway was created in concrete using stencils and coloring agents.

An elaborate design was created in cement cobblestones to help direct traffic flow and parking for this New Jersey home.

Courtesy of American Builders Associates, Inc.

Paver shapes pressed in asphalt and colored to imitate the real thing are nestled in a rock-bordered driveway.

# ENTRY PATIOS

The effect of stone is created using textured and pigmented concrete.

An entryway mosaic is created using variously hued pavers.

A stunning diamond pattern in shades of red was framed by contrasting paver "cobblestones" for this impressive entryway.

Symmetry and straight lines add formality to this grand entrance.

# Multi-Level Walks

A series of stepped circles and a matching paver walk and drive draw lots of compliments for these homeowners.

Here's something you don't see too often – trees in the center of a driveway. When they mature, these landscape additions will be a godsend on a hot summer day. Another nice addition is a cascading entry walk.

A concrete walkway is punctuated by a small patio. Here one might pause and ponder which way to step down.

Zigs and zags break up the walk from driveway to door.

Offset steps add interest as they climb to a circular patio/porch entrance. The concrete "stones" have been weathered or antiqued to create the impression that this entryway has served the home for half a century. The retaining wall blocks were color-matched, adding to the impression that this is natural stone.

Two simple cascading circles in "stone" pavers add architectural interest to this entrance.

# Hill Climbers

A rough stone retaining wall and unevenly sized flagstones lend rustic charm to this garden path.

**PREVIOUS PAGE AND THIS PAGE**
These homeowners shunned the look of concrete sidewalk with a sumptuous brick paver path that wends its way between walls to their front door.

Courtesy of the Masonry Institute Inc.

Rounded edges and a pressed surface create the effect of enormous stones in this concrete walkway.

Courtesy of Portland Cement Association

Real rock borders neatly contain cement "stone" steps.

A bewitching set of switchbacks adds interest and landscaping opportunities along these pretty steps.

**OPPOSITE PAGE**
Concrete steps imitate stone, and color coordinate with pavers in a walkway designed to harmonize with nature.

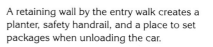

A retaining wall by the entry walk creates a planter, safety handrail, and a place to set packages when unloading the car.

Paver stones and bricks march solidly up to this front door, their color mirroring the stones in the house.

Courtesy of Interlocking Concrete Pavement Institute

A series of circles were laid in pavers for unique front and side approaches to this home.

In re-landscaping their front yard, the homeowners chose matching retaining wall block and pavers to trim the asphalt driveway and form the gently climbing staircase to their front door.

Pavers were cut to accommodate natural boulders in a walkway that negotiates a steep hill. Wrought iron railings add a measure of safety, a lot of style.

Photography by Susan Palcko/Courtesy of Pavemaster

# Straight Path

Courtesy of Vengeance Creek Stone

Here's a start to an enchanting home entrance, newly landscaped. A small spring in a stone circle matches walk and porch. Though it's not much, the little strip of stone skirt creates a perch where one can rest and enjoy the sound of bubbling water and enjoy the blooms.

Three tones were used in this intricately patterned walkway, including a
border of cement pavers that imitates granite.

Raised flower beds are easily accessed, with seating created on top of a small retaining wall. Pavers in a seemingly random pattern blend with the grays of the retaining wall and create an attractive walkway in front of the home.

Courtesy of American Builders Associates, Inc.

A formal walkway was created using angles and traditional colors, created in cast concrete.

Courtesy of Artcrete, Inc.

Courtesy of American Builders Associates, Inc.

Unique paver shapes add interest to this short walk from drive to door.

Courtesy of Superlight Block

The color will fool you: this driveway and front garden patio were sculpted in asphalt.

Straight lines and sharp angles mimic the style of this Southwestern home, and the deep blend of the pavers contrast pleasingly with the white stucco of home and wall.

# THE INDIRECT ROUTE

A curving walk works its way gently from driveway to door, allowing space for flowers and shrubs to soften the front of the home.

A gently curved walkway of imprinted concrete creates the illusion of stone, without the dangers that stone's uneven surfaces can pose.

Courtesy of Unilock

Careful calculations were used to create this mix of flagstone border and antiqued cobblestone (all concrete products) for this artful entrance walkway.

"Flagstones" of pigmented concrete lead one up this inviting shady path to a front door.

Here's a whopper of an entryway: brick walks and walls, stout columns, and brass lampposts lead to a home of equal solidity and style.

Pavers are laid end to end for a curvilinear effect. The curves are achieved by leaving small gaps as the bricks "bend." For more severe curves, bricks can be hand cut.

A stamped concrete walk sets the shape for sunny flowerbeds that guide one toward a friendly front porch.

Mortared brick pavers set in traditional, staggered rows, create a classic entry walk.

A winding path adds the illusion of length to this walkway, built of brick pavers colored to match the home.

Antiqued pavers were used to create an impression of age for this winding front walkway.

**OPPOSITE PAGE**
An entrenched garden path was sunk between walls of stone and paved with pink cobblestones. Besides the walk itself, the destination might be seating under a shady wood arbor, or the back gate beyond.

A grid of natural stone walk entices one to get out and enjoy the garden.

# Limited Access

Imprinted concrete in a slate pattern adds to the charm of this well-executed entryway, made more memorable by a wrought iron gate that mirrors arched windows surrounding the door.

Pavers picked to match a pretty stone wall create a small landing outside a courtyard gate.

Natural stone leads one down what seems
like a fairytale path under looming trees in
front of this home.

Courtesy of L.A. Verruni Landscaping

Courtesy of Unilock

Various sizes of pavers were used in this pretty
curve of walkway.

A pretty arbor over the gate creates an
enchanting entrance along this cobblestone paver walk.

# Architectural Detailing

An aerial view encompasses the unique planning and design that went into this integrated walkway, patio, and planter beds between the house and the garage.

Courtesy of Unilock

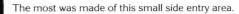
The most was made of this small side entry area.

An arch in two tones was laid in pavers to mark the transition from driveway to front entry walk.

Most people would turn their nose up at the idea of continuing asphalt from the driveway to the front door. But when it is gussied up using imprinting techniques and color sealers, the trompe l'oeil effect of pavers makes asphalt the envy of the neighborhood.

Colorful flagstones create a bright path to this handsome brick and stone home.

# Resource Guide

The following is a list of organizations and companies that contributed information and images for this book. There are several trade organizations listed that would happily help you find paving product manufacturers and suppliers, as well as certified, reliable installers in your area.

American Builders Associates, Inc.
540 Westwood Avenue
River Vale, NJ 07675
201-722-8794/Fax: 722-1457
Company president William Kirby has been installing concrete pavers in New Jersey and New York since 1985, working on large commercial projects as well as custom-designed residential applications. He is trained and certified as an ICPI interlocking paving contractor, an Anchor Paving Stone Installer, and a Keystone Retaining Wall Builder.

Artcrete, Inc.
5812 Hwy. 4 94
Natchitoches, LA 71457
318-379-2000/Fax: 379-1000
artcrete@cp-tel.net
www.artcrete.com
Artcrete manufactures stencils and products for decorative concrete under the name Faux Brick. The company has been in business for 14 years, and is represented on every continent except Greenland and the poles.

Bomanite Corporation
P.O. Box 599
Madera, CA 93639
559-673-2411/Fax: 673-8246
www.bomanite.com
e-mail: bomanite@bomanite.com
Established in 1955, Brad Bowman developed the Bomanite process of imprinting concrete. In 1970, Bomanite Corporation was established to develop a national market and installation standard for his technique. There are now 114 franchise operations in the United States and Canada, and more than 250 various types of international licensees in 66 countries worldwide.

Decorative Concrete Council
7824 South Adams Street
Darien, IL 60561
630-852-5505/Fax: 630-960-9101
plrgraphix@aol.com
www.decorativeconcretecouncil.org
A council within the American Society of Concrete Contractors, the Decorative Concrete Council works within the industry to advance the quality and use of decorative concrete systems.

Gappsi™, Inc.
311 Veterans Memorial Highway
Commack, NY 11725
631-543-1177/Fax: 543-1188
info@gappsi.com
www.gappsi.com
Owner Giuseppe Abbrancati brought his artistry and over 17 years of experience in Europe to bear when he established his company. He is the inventor of what he calls "the most reliable edge restraint system in the industry," and he has created and patented his own paver shapes for exclusive manufacture. His work has won numerous awards.

Greenridge Landscaping
14 Minnesota Road
Carbondale, IL 62901
618-549-6165/Fax: 457-4367
arobin@midwest.net
Landscape contractor Andrew Robinson has more than 20 years of experience. He specializes in custom residential landscaping.

Interlocking Concrete Pavement Institute
1444 I Street NW, Suite 700
Washington, D.C. 20005-2210
202-712-9036/Fax: 408-0285
icpi@icpi.org
www.icpi.org
The Interlocking Concrete Pavement Institute (ICPI) is an autonomous association representing the interlocking concrete paving industry in North America. Membership is open to producers, contractors, suppliers, and consultants. As the industry voice, the membership represents a majority of the concrete paver production in North America.

IXL Industries, Ltd.
Clay Products Division
P.O. Box 70
Medicine Hat, AB TIA 7E7
Canada
403-502-1486/Fax: 526-7680
www.ixlbrick.com
Known as "The Brick People," IXL is versatile, supplying a wide variety of colors, textures, and sizes of brick for commercial, institutional, and residential projects. It is a family-owned company in its third generation.

L.A. Verruni Landscaping
1357 Farmington Avenue
Pottstown, PA 19464
610-489-4389/Fax: 327-2622
santa35031@aol.com
In business for 14 years, landscape contractors Lisa and Bob Bickel specialize in installation of brick pavers and retaining walls. They are ICPI certified.

Masonry Institute Inc.
4853 Cordell Avenue
Penthouse One
Bethesda, MD 20814-3031
301-652-0115/Fax: 907-4922
www.brickblockandtrowel.org
John F. Cissel, Executive Director
Founded in 1955, The Masonry Institute, Inc. is the oldest regional masonry trade association. It promotes the use of masonry products in the Washington, D.C., metropolitan area.

New York Quarries
P.O. Box 43 Route 111
Alcove, NY 12007
518-756-3138/Fax: 756-8000
Owned and operated by the O'Brien family for three generations, New York Quarries has been supplying, fabricating, and installing natural stone for residential and commercial use since 1948; including building and landscaping for interior and exterior applications.

Pavemaster Corporation
P.O. Box 1051
1001 Skippack Pike
Blue Bell, PA 19422
215-591-9134/Fax: 591-9135
paving@pavemaster.com
In business for five years, Pavemaster specializes in interlocking pavers, modular retaining walls, and hot-mix asphalt driveways and parking lots.

Portland Cement Association
5420 Old Orchard Road
Skokie, IL 60077
847-966-6200/Fax: 966-8389
www.portcement.org
The majority of common-usage cement in the United States is portland cement. The PCA conducts research, market development, and educational work on behalf of its members – cement manufacturers in the United States and Canada. PCA programs seek to improve concrete and concrete construction and to ensure concrete's use in an ever-growing range of applications.

Regency Landscape
P.O. Box 224
Millington, NJ 07946
908-647-3434/Fax: 561-0605
regland@gateway.net
Company president Tony Catanzaro has an A.S.S. in landscape management/design; is a C.L.T. certified landscape technician by the Associated Landscape Contractors of America; a certified interlocking concrete paver installer, and has certificates from Rutgers University in landscape design and other related topics, in addition to fourteen years of industry experience.

Sterling Landscape
1081 N. Mitchell
Boise, ID 83704-8165
208-322-4505/Fax: 322-4515
bdial@sterlinglandscape.com
www.sterlinglandscape.com
Manager and designer Bill Dial, ASLA, is a registered landscape architect. The firm specializes in landscape design, construction, irrigation, and landscape management.

Superlight Block
4150 W. Turney
Phoenix, AZ 85019
800-366-7877/Fax: 602-352-3813
www.superliteblock.com
www.belgardhardscapes.com
www.oldcastle.com
Superlite is one of a network of companies across the country owned by Oldcastle, Inc., that provides a wide range of masonry products and hardscape materials to the architectural design and construction communities.

Vengeance Creek Stone
9289 W. U.S. Hwy. 64
Murphy, NC 28906
800-295-6023
vcstone@grove.net
www.vcstone.com
Supplying metamorphic quartzite – the hardest building stone in the world – mined in the Southern Appalachian Mountains of North Carolina. This quartzite can be split by hand and is prized for its durability and rich natural colors. It won't fade, flake, or chip.

StreetPrint™
Unit 102 17957 55th Avenue
Surrey, BC Canada V3S 6C4
800-688-5652/Fax: 574-7520
www.streetprint.com
A division of Integrated Paving Concepts, Inc., StreetPrint™ Pavement Texturing imprints and coats asphalt to replicate the appearance of hand-laid brick or cobblestone (in eight template styles). Templates are placed on the surface of the hot asphalt after final compaction or after reheating an existing surface that is in good condition. The StreetBond™ Surfacing System is an acrylic-polymer surfacing product with a built-in sealing element, available in ten standard colors.

Unilock, Ltd.
287 Armstrong Ave.
Georgetown, ON L7G 4X6
905-874-0312/Fax: 874-3034
www.unilock.com
Over 25 years ago, Unilock® introduced concrete paving stone to North America and continues to lead the industry in product innovation and the development.